Experiment with Photosynthesis

Nadia Higgins

Lerner Publications

Minneapolis

Lerner Publications Company
A division of Lerner Publishing Group, Inc.
241 First Avenue North
Minneapolis, MN 55401 USA

For reading levels and more information, look up this title at www.lernerbooks.com.

Library of Congress Cataloging-in-Publication Data

Higgins, Nadia.
    Experiment with photosynthesis / by Nadia Higgins.
        pages cm. — (Lightning Bolt Books™ — Plant Experiments)
    Includes index.
    ISBN 978-1-4677-5732-4 (lib. bdgs. : alk. paper)
    ISBN 978-1-4677-6075-1 (pbk.)
    ISBN 978-1-4677-6245-8 (EB pdf)
    1. Photosynthesis—Experiments--Juvenile literature. 2. Plants—Experiments—Juvenile literature. I. Title. II. Series: Lightning bolt books. Plant experiments.
    QK882.H54 2015
    572'.46—dc23   2014025221

Manufactured in the United States of America
1 – BP – 12/31/14

Table of Contents

What Happens When You Cover Part of a Leaf?

Plants cannot move from one place to another. They cannot hunt or graze. So how do plants get food to help them grow and bloom? They make their own food through photosynthesis.

An apple tree's leaves make the sugar that sweetens the fruit.

That food is actually sugar. Plants need three ingredients to make sugar. They need sunlight, water, and carbon dioxide.

A tree takes in water through the roots. The water travels through tubes in the trunk up to the leaves.

Carbon dioxide and oxygen move in and out through tiny holes in leaves.

Plants take in carbon dioxide from the air. As plants make food, they also give off oxygen.

Scientists call photosynthesis the most important process on Earth. It's why so many plants are good to eat. It's why we have oxygen to breathe.

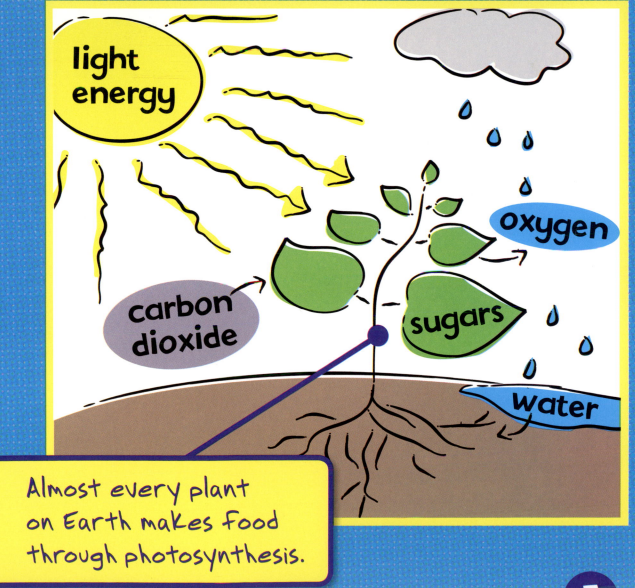

Almost every plant on Earth makes food through photosynthesis.

What happens when you take away an ingredient used in photosynthesis? Let's find out!

What You Need:

A geranium plant works well for this experiment.

plant with large leaves

black construction paper

scissors

paper clips

Steps:

1. Cut out a few shapes from the construction paper.

2. Use the paper clips to attach the shapes to the tops of some of the plant's leaves.

Make sure your shapes are smaller than the leaves. Simple shapes work best.

9

3. Put your plant in a sunny spot. Keep the soil moist for the next week.

4. Remove the patches after one week.

What do you see on the leaves after you remove the patches?

Think It Through

The part of the leaves under the shapes turned yellow. Photosynthesis could not take place. It can happen only with sunlight. If you put your plant in the light after you remove the shapes, its leaves will turn green again.

Without light, leaves cannot make food.

What Kind of Light Grows the Best Beans?

We know leaves need sunlight to stay green and make food. But not all light is the same.

Green leaves are a sign that a plant is getting enough sunlight.

What kind of light is best for plants? This experiment will help you find out!

What You Need:

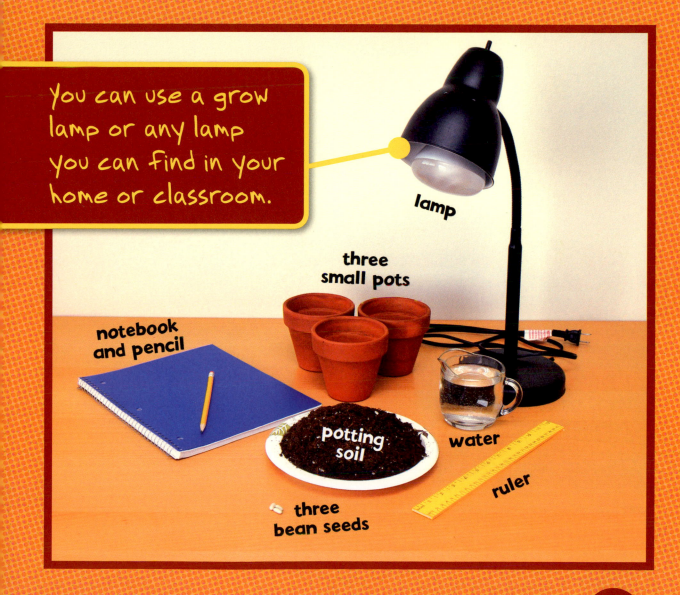

You can use a grow lamp or any lamp you can find in your home or classroom.

lamp

three small pots

notebook and pencil

potting soil

water

three bean seeds

ruler

Steps:

1. Fill each pot halfway with potting soil.

2. In each pot, push a seed about 1 inch (2.5 centimeters) under the soil.

Soon the bean seeds will start to sprout.

14

3. Add water until the soil is moist all the way through.

4. Put one pot by a sunny window. Put another under the lamp. The third pot goes in a dark cupboard.

5. Keep the soil moist in all three pots.

Check your seeds once each week over the next two weeks.

6. After two weeks, measure any stems that poke through. Count the number of leaves. Make a chart comparing stem height and the number of leaves.

Label the rows in your chart "Sunny Window," "Lamp," and "Cupboard." The columns are marked "Stem height" and "Number of leaves."

Sunlight combines all the colors of the rainbow. Indoor light is not as complete.

Think It Through

Seeds do not need light to sprout. But young plants do need light to turn green, make food, and grow. Indoor light may help, but sunlight works best.

17

What Makes Plants Green?

Chlorophyll plays a special role in photosynthesis. It acts like a kitchen stove inside a plant's cell. Chlorophyll soaks in sunlight. Then it uses energy, along with water and carbon dioxide, to make sugar.

As autumn days get shorter, trees stop making chlorophyll. The leaves change to their natural oranges and reds.

Let's take a closer look at chlorophyll.

What You Need:

fingernail polish remover

coffee filter

clear jar

pencil

tape

handful of green leaves

scissors

Steps:

1. Use the scissors to cut the green leaves into small pieces.

2. Put the leaves in the bottom of the jar. Then add fingernail polish remover.

Be sure all the leaves are covered.

3. Use the scissors to cut a strip from the coffee filter.

4. Wrap one end of the strip around the pencil.

Tape the strip in place.

5. Balance the pencil across the jar, so the strip dips into the fingernail polish remover.

6. Check your experiment each hour for five hours.

What do you see?

Plant cells store chlorophyll in special structures called chloroplasts.

Think It Through

The chlorophyll moves up the coffee filter, making it green. Chlorophyll makes leaves green too. Whenever you see green leaves in sunshine, photosynthesis is taking place.

Can a Lettuce Leaf Make Oxygen?

Almost all living things need oxygen to survive. Luckily, photosynthesis supplies our planet with this necessary gas. As green leaves make food, they also make oxygen.

Plants give off oxygen that we breathe. Plants take in carbon dioxide that we breathe out.

Let's test a lettuce leaf to see if it will make oxygen.

What You Need:

plastic cling wrap

clear jar

water

rubber band

lettuce leaf

Steps:

1. Fill the jar with water.

2. Put the leaf in the jar and cover the jar with **plastic wrap**. Place the rubber band around the jar.

Put the jar in a sunny window.

3. Predict what you will see in one hour.

4. Check the jar after one hour. Look closely. What do you see?

Tiny oxygen bubbles cling to the lettuce.

Think It Through

The oxygen bubbles were created as the leaf made food. Try the experiment with a new lettuce leaf. This time, watch the jar for one day. What do you predict will happen?

Predict Like a Scientist

Experiments start with a question—for example, "Can a plant get too much sunlight?" The next step is to answer that question. To start, make a hypothesis. Here's how:

1. Think, *Why?* Why might it be that a plant could get too much sunlight?

2. Be specific. What kind of plant might be harmed from too much light?

3. Think, *How?* How can you test your prediction with an experiment?

4. Keep trying. Don't change your prediction if it's not working. Keep observing and taking notes. You'll gain valuable facts for your next experiment.

Fun Facts

- Bacteria also use photosynthesis.

- Different kinds of plants make different kinds of sugar.

- *Photo* means "light." *Synthesis* means "putting together." *Photosynthesis* means "making with light."

- Photosynthesis has been taking place for about 2.5 billion years.

Glossary

carbon dioxide: a gas in the air that plants use during photosynthesis

cell: a microscopic building block of a living thing

chlorophyll: the green substance in a plant's leaves that absorbs sunlight

oxygen: a gas that plants give off during photosynthesis

photosynthesis: the process by which a green plant turns water and carbon dioxide into food when the plant is exposed to light

predict: to make a good guess about what might happen in the future

Further Reading

Bang, Molly, and Penny Chisholm. *Living Sunlight: How Plants Bring the Earth to Life.* New York: Blue Sky Press, 2009.

Biology4Kids.com: Photosynthesis http://www.biology4kids.com/files/plants_photosynthesis.html

Flounders, Anne. *Healthy Trees, Healthy Planet.* South Egremont, MA: Red Chair Press, 2014.

NOVA: Illuminating Photosynthesis http://www.pbs.org/wgbh/nova/nature/photosynthesis.html

TIME for Kids Big Book of Science Experiments: A Step-by-Step Guide. New York: Time Home Entertainment, 2011.

Index

Photo Acknowledgments

The images in this book are used with the permission of: © Rick Orndorf, pp. 2, 8, 9, 10, 13, 15, 16, 19, 20, 21, 22, 25, 26, 27, 30; © Alexander Chaikin/Shutterstock Images, p. 4; © 24Novembers/Shutterstock Images, p. 5; © alexpro9500/Shutterstock Images, p. 6; © davidundderriese/Shutterstock Images, p. 7; © Arina P Habich/Shutterstock Images, p. 11; © Zerber/Shutterstock Images, p. 12; © Thinkstock, pp. 14, 24, 28, 31; © S.Z./Shutterstock Images, p. 17; © Paul Paladin/Shutterstock Images, p. 18; © JaysonPhotography/Shutterstock Images, p. 23.

Front cover: © iStockphoto.com/adam smigielski.

Main body text set in Johann Light 30/36.